PIERCING STAR

Ibin Marriam

MAPLE
PUBLISHERS

PIERCING STAR

Copyright © Ibin Marriam (2024)

The right of Ibin Marriam to be identified as author of this work has been asserted by the author in accordance with section 77 and 78 of the Copyright, Designs and Patents Act 1988.

First Published in 2024

ISBN 978-1-83538-199-1 (Paperback)
978-1-83538-200-4 (E-Book)

Cover Design and Book Layout by:
White Magic Studios
www.whitemagicstudios.co.uk

Published by:
Maple Publishers
Fairbourne Drive, Atterbury,
Milton Keynes,
MK10 9RG, UK
www.maplepublishers.com

A CIP catalogue record for this title is available from the British Library. All rights reserved. No part of this book may be reproduced or translated by any form or by any means, electronic or mechanical, including photocopying, recording or by any information storage and retrieval system without written permission from the author.
The views expressed in this work are solely those of the author and do not necessarily reflect the views of the publisher, and the publisher hereby disclaims any responsibility for them.

Part 1
I Will Liberate the Ummah

I will join in last and go on to win the race.

I know my destiny, I will seek it to embrace.

I will live on my terms and walk at my own pace.

I will declare an all out war and turn my home into a military base.

I will tell kings and presidents to their face.

I will put nations and governments in their place.

I will bring to the enemies of humanity destruction and disgrace.

They will not know what hit them because I will not leave any trace.

Those whose policies are to divide, destabilise and displace.

I will kick them out of their palaces and keep them on the chase.

I will smoke them out of their offices, take them to courts and give them law case.

For crimes against humanity and refusing to change their ways.

I will erase discrimination on religion, colour and race.

I will liberate the Ummah and take them to the next phase.

I will sweep the world then lead mankind to conquer the space.

To shelter whoever may exist there too under my sovereignty through my mercy and grace.

Freedom

I don't take orders or follow.
I don't live in nobody's shadow.
I don't walk in anyone's footsteps even if he was a hero.
I take my own path in life even if it's all narrow.
I don't go by people's rules or law.
I am not part of the high classes or the low.
I am not above anybody or below.
I don't go with the flow.
I achieve more when I go solo.
I recover pretty quickly from any major blow.
Hardship and pain make me grow.
In my darkest moments I glide high and glow.
My freedom is the religion I hallow.
I don't care if you believe or not you are my bro.
And it's the same to me if you are black, white, brown or yellow.
I am not saying I am perfect but you will not see in me any flaw.

I travel at a very high speed and when I want slow.

No heartbreak can stop me or sorrow.

Let alone a society and its Pharaoh.

I don't mind fear, distress and things like these as long as I am on the go.

I never stand still, always proceed forward even if I have to restart from zero.

I own things or go without I don't ask or borrow.

Nor do I accept a favour or bestow.

One day will come my way a major cashflow.

I end every night looking forward to tomorrow.

But ready for it and very much in the know.

That life will always be challenging and raw.

You will reap what you sow.

And for no reason at all life will always throw.

Towards you a bullet and an arrow.

If you are lucky you'll get only the punch, the kick and the elbow.

Watch Life and learn don't worry about your hairdo.

Life will respect you if you are tough but floor you if shallow.

It's an awesome and formidable foe.

It will see everybody off whether good, bad or weirdo.

Magnificent Character

I watch my peace of mind and protect.
So when people speak their mind I don't try to correct.
I don't quarrel or object.
I don't embarrass them or upset.
I don't put anyone on the spot.
I stay away from being unpleasant.
I don't insult their intellect.
I don't challenge them or confront.
I don't dismiss what they say or suspect.
I try to give them the benefit of doubt.
I don't wanna be difficult.
Also it's damaging to your mental health if you always mistrust.
But when an idiot comes to me I send him on his way straight.
And if he refuses to go I put him in his place tight.
I don't really deal with people generally or interact.

I don't associate with anyone, not even my sect.
I don't give my opinion or suggest.
I don't wanna bring on myself anything I might regret.
When I walk the streets I don't put my foot on an insect.
To the creation of Allah I show some respect.
And when I see a spider in my bedroom I don't say pest.
It was here before me and will be after me, I am the guest.
When I put my head on the pillow I look back at the day and reflect.
I am my own judge, I bring myself to account every night.

I don't talk to anyone against their wish.
Nor do I interrupt their conversations cause that's rude and foolish.
I don't go to people to show off or try to astonish.

I don't think I am better than anybody, If I do that I will be the first to perish.

I don't support wrong doers or corrupt leaders that would bring me regret and anguish.

I just follow the Quran, it's the road to safety and to flourish.

It gives me freedom, honour and happiness so I hold on to it and cherish.

I care about all human beings, I am not a hater or selfish.

I am ready for the Hereafter cause this world will soon finish.

I don't repeat myself or swear.

I don't discuss my personal affair.

I always try to be nice to people and forbear.

Cause I know We're all humans we make mistakes here and there.

I don't look people in the eye or stare.

In my dealings I am just and fair.

I also try not to have any worry or care.

That brings only misery and despair.

I don't wanna own properties nor wanna be a millionaire.
I pass on everything I can spare.
Clearing everything off my mind allows me to be of my Lord aware.

I don't have time to disagree with people or argue.
I don't have with them any issue.
I have more important things to do.
If you don't attack me I will never attack you.

I chat with people but I don't get personal.
I always try not to get angry or emotional.
I don't criticise nor be judgemental.
To see me being rude or aggressive it's impossible.
I don't show respect to idiots even if they are rich and powerful.

I don't give advice or fatwa.
I don't waste my time on dawah.

Because I know I don't have any effect or power.

I don't use religion or politics as a net for people's money to devour.

I don't take sides in disputes.

I don't go around giving everybody the blues.

I am not opinionated so I keep to myself my views.

I always choose peace and give trouble the defuse.

Attacking someone's beliefs or culture that's something I refuse.

I treat people with respect and dignity, not how I choose.

My way is brotherhood and to carry good news.

Some people like to go around to upset others or to smear

I ignore them and keep clear.

But when threatened I stand my ground and I don't show any fear.

My humility steps aside and lets my bravery to the surface appear.

Then my spirit takes charge of me and fills the whole atmosphere.

I don't say to anyone come here.

And if someone says that to me I just pretend I didn't hear.

In people's business, freedom and rights I don't interfere.

To their personal space I don't go near.

Respect and good manners are my religion and to me very dear.

Legendary

I don't associate with anybody at all, I am solitary.

I am out of reach only available in the world of imaginary.

I am too good to be true a legendary.

The finest in mankind history extraordinary.

When it comes to preparing for the future, a visionary

For character and manners exemplary.

For justice, equality and progression sanctuary.

I am free-minded and flexible but When I stand my ground stationary.

Fear, follow, weak, worry and words like these don't exist in my dictionary.

Honour, freedom, peace, rule of law and the like of them are my vocabulary.

My knowledge and wisdom is a library.

I work in the field of literature and literary.

Piercing Star

My background is prophetic and royal pedigree.

People have no choice but to treat me as a dignitary.

Whoever talks to me has to take precautionary.

I fight a worldwide war on behalf of humanity I am revolutionary.

To the enemies of humanity a formidable adversary.

Once I set a foot on earth their rule changes from permanent to temporary.

I will stop them in their tracks and change the course of history.

I carry the hopes and dreams of humanity by compulsory.

When I take the driving seat people will enjoy life and the scenery.

For the universe to have balance, my presence in it is necessary.

I am a gift from heaven and also its secretary.

To lead mankind to their destination only by honorary.

Natural Born Rebel

They brought the ummah to the edge of a great peril.

They will not hesitate to plunder or to kill.

They turned Muslim countries into either a war-zone or a stable.

They disabled our capabilities, powers and potential.

They lead us to despair and distress on a roundabout circle.

But all that will come to a halt upon the arrival.

Of the Lone wolf and the natural born rebel.

Soon I will be gliding down from my dangerous level.

To send these herders back to their camel.

To neutralise satans I will have to temporarily become the devil.

I will free the ummah and lead them on the great struggle.

Where one drop of Muslim blood shed will mean the army to assemble.

They will kill you in your home so you might as well just die in the battle.

They shell our homes and bury our families under the rubble.

If you don't defend the Muslims, you're not a Muslim pure and simple.

Never live on your knees or let them impose on you their will.

Unless we eliminate them, we'll never ever be able to settle.

They waged war on us and made it total.

So fighting back is a command from Allah not optional.

Lone Wolf

I will put this world in order.

I am not very far from the divine border.

I am the justice upholder.

Every day I grow bolder and bolder.

I carry the whole universe on my shoulder.

I get younger and stronger with time, people get weaker and older.

The globe without me is in disarray and disorder.

I am the best ever and the record holder.

The honour of the world and its mysterious wonder.

A lone wolf who just likes to wander.

I neutralise human rights abusers in a blood that goes for them colder and colder.

I am made of fire, dynamite and gun powder.

The human intellect can't measure me nor about me ponder.

When I open my mouth ignorant wrong doers hear nothing but thunder.

And if they come to face me on the battlefield and not surrender.

They will be the ones who will go under.

There I become a killing machine I don't play or plunder.

I don't accept crimes against humanity even a slander.

I lead the fight from front even though I am His Majesty's irreplaceable army commander.

I will usher in a new era and become an empire founder.

The truth will soon split from falsehood upon the dawn of the divider.

The eternal warrior and the night rider.

The guide and the path finder.

In this world of slaves and followers I am a free outsider.

And at the divine court a dignified insider.

The world is going nowhere without the permission of its minder.

The gap between me and mankind keeps getting wider.

But I am still the rock of my people and their provider.

10,000 years ago was the last time I made a blunder.

So don't take chances against someone who's character speaks louder.

Or challenge a flawless man who hits back harder.

I was born in the divine presence and grew up in its corridor.

And now His Majesty's man on earth and His ambassador.

The Rising Sun from the West

Allah made me the Sun which will rise from the west.

I am now oppressors's worst nightmare and everybody's ultimate test.

Like Allah said this life is a competition, it's over I've won the con-test.

God has already put everyone to rest.

But there are still few more things I want to get off my chest.

He wants me here because He wants to clean His earth of all the pest.

Satan and his associates have turned the land of Allah into an evil-infested nest.

They made themselves gods so everything they do God detest.

They took away people's freedom and added to that humiliation and insult.

If you don't do what they say they'll have you jailed and inflict you with torment.

Or you politely ask for your rights, they will sign away your life with immediate effect.

But soon they will know the power of Allah which they've been trying to forget.

He will hand-pick out of all His servants for this job the most capable and the absolute best.

An authorised individual and highly dignified already here but soon will manifest.

With my two horns I will gore to death anyone who tries to block me from my quest.

I don't tolerate transgression against me or anybody nor any disrespect.

I will do anything I please and I will not accept at all any threat.

I will put the Muslim house in order and personally press the button for a historical reset.

I will bring down high people and raise the low, all will be equal in every aspect.

I will equally distribute resources no-one will anymore suffer any neglect.

I will peacefully solve all problems and spread the culture of respect.

I will establish order, strengthen the economy, raise the living standard and give every right.

I will never leave anyone behind regardless of religion. race, language or sect.

I will bring everybody in from the cold and stand guard to serve and protect.

No-one dares come near my people as long as I am in this world present.

All humanity is my family, I am a brother to all, it will be around the world felt.

After I get my job done I will go back to my God direct.

Allah loves me and trusts me, counts on me and shows me great respect.

Every time He addresses me if He doesn't hold me I will melt.

Because the amount of honour He gives me keeps me forever to Him in debt.

I don't wanna be with people I am tired of them and their mindset.

I want to be in this world only to look after my mother and be for her a servant.

Holy Spirit Personified

Me and dictators are on course to collide.

The result for them will be a kick in the backside.

I am a man who can never ever be denied.

Actually the Holy Spirit personified.

The divine court is my military base also where I reside.

When I come down to earth I take the whole universe with me on my glide.

And when I step into the beach the ocean has no option but to divide.

Just showing up is all I need for wrongdoers to hide.

I will single handedly defeat the forces of the allied.

If anyone fights alongside me that would be for me a downside.

I own victory itself and give it to whoever I decide.

When I take the driving seat, jump in or you will be left behind.

Soon I will make my move and take the whole ummah with me on my stride.

I will be their voice, arm and mind.

I will restore for them their freedom and pride.

They will take their rightful place at the forefront of mankind.

I will close the door of Fitnah and put all differences aside.

No-one at all will be marginalised.

I will make sure every human being is honoured and dignified.

Our culture will be equality, order and being kind.

If you look for inhumanity or indecency amongst us you will never find.

The One Foretold

I am the coming man, the one foretold.

Of a lofty moral virtue admired in heaven and adored.

Authorised by the master of the universe and its Lord

In the world of fear and humiliation respected, honoured and assured.

Surrounded by danger but calm and secured.

My countenance is simply too powerful for mankind to behold.

Allah put time itself for me on hold.

He bought me and got all mankind sold,

The world without me is a very dark place and cold,

They'll get warmth and guidance only when my light unfold.

I am feared and dangerous but pro-humanity warlord.

Anyone who stands in my face will be advised to move or will be floored.

It would be a fatal mistake to use against me the sword.

I am the castle of the truth and its stronghold.

I never change my principles nor go back on my word.

With the normal people whether religious or not I am generous and pure gold.

As for violent idiots I send them to the emergency ward.

I will put an end to politicians mismanagement, corruption and fraud.

They will hear from me but if they don't do as told.

They will be shown the door or stormed.

Light of the World

When Allah and His angels look down on earth the only light they see is my light.

I avoid meeting people because for them I am way too bright.

If I don't wear my mask they will go blind outright.

They are not ready for me yet so I will wait until time is right.

Mankind can't survive for a second if they were where I am at.

So I have to come down for them because they can't reach my height.

I try not to tell them about me because they Will be lost in a world of doubt.

The knowledge they've been seeking and gathering, it's me what it's all about.

They are my pain and sometimes my delight.

They unknowingly put their sins on me, I take them away to get them wiped out.

They are my inspiration which I can't do without.

They help me with my Dunya so I help them with their Aakhirat.

They fell short on their duties so I'll do for them their Salat.

They don't have connection with the Almighty so I'll provide for them that.

Because they got on their minds everything except the one who possesses all might.

They messed up the history so I will have to come to rewrite.

They don't have courage and bravery so on their behalf I will fight.

But they need to be careful because Allah will one day get all that cut out.

He's got more important things for me to do than to get them always bailed-out.

He wants to raise me to a level and give me a glory nobody's ever heard about.

He wants me to dominate the universe and set it alight.

Emerge from it, rise above it then let it all fall apart.

Judgement Day Tower

The love of Allah is always on me like a heavy shower.

That's why I ooze freedom, honour, dignity and power.

You heard about the judgement day I am its tower.

You wanna see that for yourself then just wait for the Hour.

For people who don't have respect it's gonna be sour.

I will cut them down to their size and bring them lower.

Then offer them as food for hell to devour.

I am so generous that my relatives call me a money thrower.

I am authorised, well-informed and a knower.

I don't talk much, I am more like a doer.

A high-flying banner and evil mower.

A serious, decisive individual with willpower.

Not a player or a cinema goer.

I attract death and danger like a whistleblower.
I die when I go to bed and come back newer.
When I face armies I make them look fewer.
And when I sprint the light seems slower.

Roaring

I used to forgive idiots but not anymore.

Been always silent, one day I will roar.

Walked on the streets now I soar.

I am back for my enemies to settle the score.

They will see from me what they've never seen before.

They will be shocked to the core.

Now if they don't know their limits I will step away unscratched leaving them lying on the floor.

Heads of states can't afford to take me lightly or ignore.

If they do that it's gonna be war.

What people love, I deplore.

The things they enjoy leave me sore.

What they do for fun is a killing bore.

When I ran out of things to do for fun or to explore.

I turned to the universe to put it in order, now I got the world in my sight for some more.

I will reveal myself, it's gonna be a very heavy downpour.

I've got kindness, brotherhood and prosperity in store.

Self-belief

I am humanity's most mentally tough and only hope.

You can't come with me where I go because you will simply not be able to cope.

The smallest creature there will have you all on the rope.

He can flick earth out of its orbit with the back of his hand in one swoop.

They got all running but they know I am the only one who can step-up.

It's a place of danger where death rules, not a beauty shop.

After I wear Allah's powers, protection and love like a robe.

I go there when I want to have some fun to mess them up.

When I face them the ground underneath them knows me so it becomes a slippery slope.

They run away from me but I got them on my scope.

They spread corruption on earth but all that will end once I set foot on the globe.

I will clean this earth of them with my capabilities and my mop.

My presence on earth alone is enough to get them to stop.

If they don't my wrath will reach them and shroud them like an envelope.

They thought I'll never come but I am here and their time is up.

I am a man wherever I go things automatically go down and let me be on top.

They know who I am, if they don't act accordingly they will get the chop.

Confidence

I struggle to contain my confidence.

In my veins run freedom, dignity and independence.

I am made of steel and my character oozes magnificence.

I am where I want to be but for humanity I will go the whole distance.

I will discharge my duty and rid the world of hatred and ignorance.

I will uproot cruelty and violence.

I will lead campaigns to topple dictators and their villains.

Then sit on the throne of global governance.

I don't seek power but it's the only way to guarantee deliverance.

I will prioritise education and science.

Injustice, inhumanity and corruption will end upon my entrance.

I can do that and I don't need to show for it any evidence.

My word is the most truthful thing in existence.

I am the DNA of the ultimate truth and its essence.

This world gets its honour and meaning from my presence.

I also give humanity their light and guidance.

And life gets its beauty and elegance.

I will have on the world the greatest ever influence.

I will fight crime, eradicate drugs and the use of substance.

We will open factories, cultivate lands and reach self-sufficience.

Law will prevail in society together with conscience.

Weaker members of society will get what they need and every assistance.

Jewel in the Crown

I am a man who is free and independent.
Bold certain sure and confident.
Sharp smart wise and intelligent.
Calm cool balanced and patient.
Thinker genius planner and brilliant.
Leader guide advisor and consultant.
Dignified praised honoured and prominent.
Author writer poet and eloquent.
Soldier fighter warlord and militant.
Protector saviour defender and vigilant.
Tough strong solid and persistent.
Determined resolute decisive and resilient.
Friendly courteous gentle and pleasant.
Outstanding remarkable bright and magnificent.
Straight frank clear and consistent.
Charismatic rebel revolutionary and dissident.
Favoured chosen exempted and important.
Hopeful dreamer optimistic and passionate.
Cultured educated civilised and considerate.

The Flood of Allah

I am the Flood of Allah and also His stronghold.

One day He will unleash me and I will overwhelm the whole world.

Sooner or later I will stand up and when I do.

Allah will stand up too.

I don't kill, destroy nor harm,

I just manoeuvre my way around.

I do not have problems with people nor hold a grudge.

I just get them out of my way to proceed forward.

Allah loves me and trusts me, counts on me and respects me.

So eat your heart out my enemy.

He doesn't give me an order He inspires me.

And will not spare anything to hire me.

I am Elevated Authorised, Venerated Justified, Enabled Mystified, Revered Dignified, Feared

Magnified, Respected Glorified.

He is my will and I am His fearlessness.

Ibin Marriam

He is my patience and I am His decisiveness.

He is my intelligence and I am His bravery.

He is my knowledge and I His oratory.

When people see me they remember Him so talking to me is a minor Salat for them.

When Allah wants to tell me something He just tells Himself and when I want to tell Him

something I just tell myself.

And when mankind tells us something we just throw it on the shelf.

He put me on earth to see Himself.

don't even contemplate that, it's out of your depth.

I don't sleep and wake up when I go to bed.

I die and come back from the dead.

The rich and powerful speak to me the way their servants speak to them.

Because they see me walking with my feet firmly on earth and my head in the seventh heaven.

The sun always salutes me and asks for my permission before it set or rise.

Also animals, birds, insects, clouds and everything salute me when they pass by.

As for paradise.

I just go there I don't hope or fantasise.

And the hell you fear I also go there when I feel like it.

Because when it sees me it chills out and puts its fire behind it.

He is Tough

He is the face and I am the mask.

He paves the way for me to glory and at the same time got my back.

He is above mankind and I am below.

Together we surround them, there's no escape for them, nowhere to go.

He drives them from the back and in front I lie low.

He created me to meet Satan's challenge and also for the angels to see Him in a way they never saw Him before.

His out-of-this-world high standard is very demanding.

He wants to give me a magnificent character and to also be in it commanding.

He is tough with me to make me to the people lenient.

He always keeps me in line whether I like it or not.

I carry Him and carry me.

And when I die He will be the one who will pray on me and bury me.

Allah is the only one who defeated me and humbled me.

The only one who outsmarted me and baffled me.

So when I see Him coming I run for cover.

Cause I know what He is capable of I don't run from no other.

If I do that He'll disown me and bar me from seeing Him forever.

Shirk

When Allah said don't be of the mushrikeen.

He is here talking about worshipping the Deen.

He is talking here about taking part in what people do in their lives.

Stay away from their Dunya affairs if you want to survive.

Or if you take orders from any people.

Then you're definitely a mushrik because you're feeble.

How can you be weak like this?

When you are with the almighty Himself and His angels.

Sort that out right now because death is coming soon.

Or you will find yourself in the Hereafter and amongst the mushrikoon.

If governments and their heads of states.

Interfere in the business and the affairs.

Of a real Muslim or just speak to him without his permission.

The pillars of their kingdoms and republics will be shaken.

You're not dealing here with any geezer.

Watch out! Knight Templar.

You're dealing with someone who is dealing with Allah.

He is someone spiritually connected in a very powerful way.

Everything in the universe runs according to his feelings and thoughts every day.

If you think people can't do without you in both Dunya and religion.

Then you are a cursed Satan.

So just leave us alone Mr superstar.

And go away from us somewhere very far.

A real Muslim only minds his own business and most humble.

He hates to even be noticed while walking the streets, if that happens it would be enough to make him crumble.

(Part 2)
A Statement of Serious Gravity

Being spiritually gifted made me the highest man in existence today and I am not even done yet, Allah will raise me even higher and I will not stop until I reach a level that has never been reached before.

I don't exist in the universe, the universe exists in me.

I've got the seven heavens in my right pocket, the seven earths in my left and the universe in my back pocket.

The sun goes out from me and comes back down in me, the moon rotates around me, I made this world my footwear, I placed paradise to my right and hell to my left, the angels are behind me and mankind in front of me and Allah Himself sitting on the throne of my heart resuming authority in full control with absolute power reigning from within me down below on earth just like He always reigned from heaven above without. I am His man on earth just like He is my God in heaven.

I am His warning and also His good news.

He will send me against the world to put nations in their place.

I don't know how people can know Him without me.

I've made the greatest comeback ever done in mankind history and it will trigger the comeback of the Ummah, my resurrection will ignite theirs,

I will unite them and put them back on track to their glory,

I will give them their golden age once more.

I will volunteer to take up the place of the prophet Muhammad amongst the Ummah while taking into consideration the differences' because the Ummah needs its finest to step forward and take up leadership to get the balance right and navigate the Islamic ship to safety through rising oceans, hurricanes and stormy weather.

Only someone who managed to safely reach his own final destination can get them to theirs safely.

They need someone prepared and experienced who knows what he's doing, knows when to take risks and ignore dangers for this worthiest of causes.

A brother who listens, who will do for them what they want not what he wants, who loves and serves them and also fair with his opponents.

They need someone who freed himself by smashing his own shackles to break theirs to free them then enable them to go on to take their rightful place amongst the nations. I will do the impossible by getting the massive Muslim train which has been stalled for centuries moving again to its destination.

No-one I ever confronted but eventually chose to be my friend because they realise at the end I am someone they don't want to be on bad terms with.

My friendship is everyone's gain and the lack of it is their loss.

God might pardon everyone because of me, because their fate is not a priority to Him and me after all.

Let it Rain

My emergence is the reason why mankind was created.

I am the first at the forefront of mankind.

I am so high I can afford to come down.

So rich and wealthy I can afford to live in poverty.

Very powerful and capable, I can afford weakness and helplessness.

I am so knowledgeable I want to be ignorant about everybody and everything. I command huge armies that wait for a nod from me yet I go to danger on my own.

Unreachable I can afford to make dangerous areas my home.

Strong and healthy beyond all boundaries that's why I like to spend ages on a hospital bed from time to time to relieve my boredom.

Dignified beyond all measures, I am unhumiliateable.

I am so smart and intelligent I play dumb sometimes to preserve my energy and maintain my good mood.

I am an intellectual thinker but I don't wanna be known for it, I don't wanna lose the blessings and the freedom of being unknown.

I am an undercover agent.

I gave up a lot of my powers and capabilities to be able to get the freedom to do the simplest things in life which are the greatest blessings like going out and about and walking the streets in peace.

I am a visionary, before I decide on a matter or make a move I look at the far future beyond thousands of years.

I am steeped in history before I take one step forward, I look back in history thousands of years.

I ooze happiness and joy that's why I pass it all to my parents, relatives, friends and anyone who asks me and I take their misery, distress and pain.

To pass an exam I don't need to answer right I just put my signature to it and it will be passed, that's why I take for my people anything that they can't pass.

I Feel So Fine

Allah made me paralyzed by making me feel the way He feels but still it feels so fine. He said to me take your rightful place in the universe and live life according to our terms. Feel the way I do and always think like this, it's your fuel, High ranking Honour and Defence mechanism.

I ooze confidence, fearlessness, freedom, dignity and honour.

I am the gate where Allah's powers and capabilities come to this world through.

What keeps the world and everything in it going is the energy that emits from me.

If I fail mankind fail, if I succeed they succeed.

They are not allowed to move forward one inch until I move forward.

I am the one who when I appear the universe disappears.

When I am about to move the universe braces itself.

I top the sky in highness.

I dwarf the mountains.

My light eclipses the sun.

My coolness will put out hell's fire.

I am so dangerous even I am scared of me.

When I take a bullet the bullet dies.

I am so dignified owning anything or having servants is below me.

I am so great I know everything about everybody and everything but I don't know everything about Myself.

I am heavier than the universe, I don't even know how I am moving.

I know everything but I prefer to be without knowledge to have some fun. I am so powerful even my enemies work and fight for me.

Everything's existence depends on me.

My religion is holiness, I am so holy only me is good enough to worship me. If I say a lie it becomes absolute truth as soon as it comes out of my mouth. I am above death, I am the one who will make death die. Everything in existence prays that they don't come to my attention because if they do it could be the end of them. They wait for ages in hope that I honour them by allowing them to be in my presence. Everything is not enough for me.

I am so holy it is forbidden to worship me and it's a sin to mention my name. I hide myself because I don't want to be worshipped. Complements are out right aggression against me. If someone calls me I wonder how they dared to call me.

If they talk to me I forgive them because they don't know that what they did could bring them serious harm.

If I put a price for people for a chance to speak to me it would be their lives.

The only thing that is allowed for people in my presence is for them to be non-existent.

When I say a word the only ear that deserves the honour of hearing it is mine. I am so great I am out of reach for mankind only me is worthy of my company. If I want something it comes running looking for me.

If anyone or anything waits until I have to say what I want from them they know they will have to seize to exist and be replaced.

Even myself is not allowed to discuss my own affairs with me.

If I want something from the universe but can't deliver, it seizes to exist and another universe has to come into existence to deliver.

Nice to meet you, I told you I feel so fine.

I Rank So High

I Rank so High only Allah is above me.

Can you live like you are the only human being on earth?

Can you live according to the contradicting realities and rules of this world and the Hereafter at the same time?

Can you survive a decade of lack of interest in life, deleted knowledge, loss of memory, perpetual and continuous States of being paralyzed by not being sure about anything to do including the simplest things in life like entering a shop or walking on the street, a state where you don't know whether you're coming or going, in or out, right or wrong, where you will also find fear suddenly descended on you so much so even your shadow scares you. Can you do your part and the parts of many others without complaining? Can you keep Allah on your mind every second 24-7?

Can you work for Allah for nothing then pay to continue working for Him?

Can you know what Allah wants, what He means when He says something?

Can you speak His language?

Can you stop living your life and start living His?

Allah doesn't eat, drink, sleep or worry can you do that?

He doesn't have a father, mother, brother, sister, son, daughter, friends or country, can you be like that?

He doesn't allow anybody to speak to Him without permission, and when He allows them He doesn't accept things like suggesting things to Him, saying the word no to Him, asking or begging Him for anything, can you be like that with people?

Can you fly in the domain of His level?

Can you represent Him on earth?

Can you go near Him without getting killed by the dangers He surrounded Himself with?

Can you survive if He gives you the ability to see things the way He sees them and feel the way He does and still do as He expects you?

If He gives you His will can you use it the right way?

If He sits you on His throne can you keep His kingdom going alright without major problems?

If He lets you walk with Him can you keep up?

If He takes you somewhere and leaves, can you find your way back to Him and in one piece?

Can you solve the puzzles He gives you or who's your god and how does he treat you?

Dangerous Level of Freedom

On this level I broke out of humanity, I hover over them.

I venerate and revere myself.

I am the one and only nobody exists beside me.

I direct the momentum to come my way.

I don't need to do, have or be anything in this world, I do that in the real world as far as I am concerned within my mind.

I dismiss the rich and powerful together with the scum, the people I know and those I don't and for no particular reason.

When it comes to manners and character only mad people or people who don't know who I am will try to compete with me.

People would like to speak to me but they change their minds out of fear bordering respect. I allow people to speak to me only if they know their place with me.

I normally avoid getting into an intellectual discussion with anybody because it's not good for them.

I don't pray for myself or ask for forgiveness. Angels, birds, animals, fish, insects and the whole creation of Allah do that for me.

The Demands of the Ummah to the Leaders

Get the Ummah United regardless of sect.

Establish military alliances and financial and social ties between Muslim countries. Up hold the spirit and the principles of Islam.

Put in place an independent justice system.

Put an end to the theft and abuse of public money.

Allow rights and freedoms which don't go against the spirit and teachings of Islam.

Bring in free and fair elections.

Abolish the position of Mufti and don't interfere in the affairs of the scholars so that they could do their job properly.

Running for Khalifa (Caliph)

Allah said in the Quran about the true believers (those who pray and say our Lord make us leaders of the believers)

And the prophet said (Every Muslim has the right to lead and to represent the ummah) He also said (anyone who dies without swearing allegiance to a true Muslim leader will die as a non-Muslim).

I will unite the Ummah.

I will leave each sect to follow its doctrine or school of thought.

I will put an end to their inner fighting.

I Will peacefully solve all the problems between them.

I will not allow the west or anyone to militarily attack any Muslim country or continue to plunder our resources.

I will not allow anyone to interfere into the political and religious affairs of the Ummah.

I will bring back true brotherhood between all Muslims despite their many differences in sects, race, language etc.

I will establish equality and rule of law and I will spread the culture of respect for all regardless of religion, sects etc.

I will give people stability, order and security.

I will strengthen the economy, raise the living standard, distribute the wealth equally, nobody will be left behind.

I will give all their complete freedom and rights.

No-one will need to migrate to the west or even leave their own country for economic or security reasons.

There will be no more torture in prisons, a police officer will not be allowed to lay a finger on anyone or insult them at all, no-one will be arrested unless there's a strong evidence or valid reason.

Religious leaders will not be allowed to interfere in politics, running the affairs of the country will be left to politicians.

There will be no intelligence agency that spies on the public, it will be directed to fight crime.

Belief or lack of it will be made a personal thing between the individual and God, no-one will be oppressed or discriminated against in any way shape or form because they don't believe.

I will sort out the Israel issue.

(Part 3)
Allah and me

Allah sends only me into situations that demand His presence.

He is my judge and I am His executioner, He is my safety and I am His adventure, He is my home and I am His military base, He is my faith and I am His confidence, He is my power and I am His fame, He is my tribal chief and I am His clansman, He is my marshall and I am His soldier, but when He fights I become His weapon His shield and where He shoots from. I seek Him but He finds me.

I die for Him and He lives for me, I lose for Him and He wins for me, I fight for Him and He prevails for me, I work for Him and He achieves for me, I look for Him and He sees for me, I talk to Him and He speaks for me,

The door of my world is open for Him He is welcome to come in anytime He wants, when I am in or not, and the door of His world is open for me He welcomes me anytime I want to come.

People go against His will and I swim alongside it, He sends against them storms, and shower me with His love, they drown in the lake of His anger and I dive in the ocean of His favour.

People who know me call me soldier, Allah named me Mahmood and Gabriel calls me Ibin Marriam.

It's enough for the Devil to send to you his smallest soldier to destroy you but I forced him out of his throne to come to me himself and still couldn't do anything. Jesus will kill the Dajjal and it's me who will kill the Devil.

Muslims ask me to come to their mosques, I could go, it's not a problem but if they knew I have a Maqam (Stand) they wouldn't have asked.

They ask me don't you follow the Quran? They don't know I became the Quran.

They also ask, are you not a Muslim? I resist the desire to tell them I am Islam itself.

I can't find a way to tell them that I reached the level where my religion now is Fitrah (Holiness or Natural Disposition. Being always exactly the way God wants you to be).

When people talk to me Allah writes in my heart what I need to say to reply. I am the shadow of Allah, He deals with me and might let you deal with His shadow. If you hate Him you will hate me and if you disrespect me you will disrespect Him. I am His biggest sign of His existence.

When people see me they remember Him so talking to me is a minor salat for them. He gave people their religions and gave me His Deen, He gave them their laws and gave me His own law that He goes by, He gives me what He gives Himself and He gives them what He wants to throw away, He gives them what they want to get rid of them and gives me what makes me stay with Him.

When I am with people and we separate they go home with each other or separately but He comes home with me.

People every day go back home to their families and I go home to Him. You might ask Him to give you an order, He will tell you to do something that's not important to Him but when He wants something important done He whispers it to my ear and inspires me.

Allah Loves me

Allah loves me and trusts me, He counts on me and respects me, He doesn't give me an order He inspires me, He doesn't command me He suggests things to me, He treats me the way He treats Himself, He doesn't talk to me He whispers in my ear and addresses me. I gave Him my name and He gave me His so when He is called I answer and when I am called He answers.

I gave Him my place and He gave me His so dealing with Him is dealing with me and dealing with me is dealing with Him.

He is on the inside and I am on the outside and sometimes I am on the inside and He is on the outside, He is above and I am below together we surround Mankind, He is in front of them and I am behind them, I test people and He punishes or rewards them. He is the power and I am the tool, He is the driver and I am the vehicle, He's in the driver's seat and I am in the passenger's next to Him and sometimes I am the driver and He is sitting next to me.

I am lost in Him and He is found in me, I am unable in Him and He is in control in me, I am dead in Him and he is alive in me, I don't exist in Him and he exists in me, I am deaf and blind in Him and He is seeing and hearing in me, People can find Him in me but they can't find me in Him.

By being lost in Him I am found and truly guided, I am exactly where I want to be, in absolute freedom, beyond good and evil, above right and wrong, happiness and sadness richness and poverty, honour and disgrace, highness and lowliness, life and death, sin and obedience, knowledge and ignorance, hell and paradise.

In Him I will never die and in me He will bring this world to an end.

I am where He wants me to be.

I realised my own day of resurrection, I got judged by God and made it to heaven, I broke into the unseen world, I exist in the stage between this world and the hereafter where I can go to heaven and this world any time I like.

I am the master of my destiny, the captain of my ship, the king of my world, the ruler of my space, the leader of my kind, the judge in my court, the sovereign of my state.

People who know me when they need something I am the first one they think about, they normally avoid me and speak only when they have to, before they speak they ask for my permission, they keep it respectful and they don't get personal, they get straight to the point because they know they only have short time with me, they choose their words carefully and they think about what they want to say before they say it, they know their limits with me and for those who don't, they'll learn, they might backbite me but no-one dares say a word in my presence, the people who know me don't only trust me they believe in me.

The Shadow of Allah

When Allah says something I give it my full unconditional backing no thinking or hesitation or consideration for anyone or anything and when I say something He gives it His full unconditional backing no consideration for anyone.

If you want to speak to me you have to go to Him first and if you want to speak to Him you have to come to me first.

If you want to fight Him you need to get rid of me first and if you want to fight me you will have to deal with Him first.

He did me a favour by bringing me to exist in this world and I returned the favour by bringing Him to exist in my heart.

I trust Him with my world and He trusts me with His kingdom, I let Him sit on my throne of my heart and He let me sit on His throne, I trust Him with my life and He trusts me with His.

I go with Him wherever He wants to go and He comes with me wherever I want to go. I believe in Him because He believes in me.

I become alive when He thinks of me and He becomes present in this world when I think of Him.

I stand for Him where He is not and He stands for me where I am not.

I represent Him on earth and He represents me in heaven.

When I walk He is my shadow and sometimes when He walks I am His shadow.

Sometimes He is the face and I am His mask and sometimes I am the face and He is my mask.

If I stand in front of a mirror He shows up and if He stands in front of a mirror I show up.

When I go to war He's got my back and when He goes to war I got His. I fight His war and He fights mine, I fight whoever He fights and He fights whoever I fight. I am His striking force on earth and He is my striking force in heaven, we are the two sides of the same coin.

I am His physical aspect and He is my spiritual aspect.

He is my Secret

He is my secret and I am His and one day both secrets will come out.

Sometimes I threaten the people by Him and sometimes He threatens them by me.

Sometimes He sends me against them and sometimes I send Him against them. Sometimes I intercede for them with Him and sometimes He intercedes for them with me. He asks me about my people on earth and I ask Him about His angels in heaven, I tell the people about Him and He tells the angels about me.

I take Him where He wants to go and He takes me where I want to go.

My will is His will and His will is my will.

Allah said to me get out of my way and when people look at you don't let them see you let them see me, when they talk to you let them talk to me, when they listen to you let them hear me, when they come to you let them deal with me.

If they hate you they think they hate you but it's me they hate not you and when they love you it's me they love not you, when they fight you it's me they fight.

He said to me when you go to the battlefield, dress for wedding because you will be thinking of me there and dancing, not distracted from me by the fighting, let the angels do the fighting.

Heavy Weight

If you put all mankind from the time of Adam till the end of days on the scale and put me on the other side I will outweigh them easily.

I am gifted and highly lifted. Raised and praised.

It's not that I hope to go to paradise or heaven I just go there whenever I want, I also go to hell when I want, I die and come back to life all the time at will, if I want something I just do it and if I don't want it I just don't do it as simple as that.

Health, illness, richness, poverty, knowledge, ignorance and all things like them are my properties, they don't happen to me because I have power over them, I am above them I go through them all the time at will, they are my fun.

I don't die, I disappear to make way for Allah to come in then Allah makes way for me to reappear.

Allah shares with me everything He has, even His name (Allah), between Him and me there is no shirk or Kufr, believe or disbelieve, good deed or bad, paradise or hell, Dunya or hereafter, to cut a long story short, nothing at all between Him and me. My life now became nothing but a permanent moment of anxious wait, where I am always bracing myself because I know that He will emerge from within me any moment now. I am not capable of love, He is, He will make me love Him, He is very generous, if you do just 1% of what He wants from you provided you try your best He will give you all these things and more.

I struggle to contain my confidence, my fearlessness scares me, the high level I am on is dizzying, the high speed I go by endangers my life, my awareness of Allah petrifies me, my knowledge silences me and my holiness isolates me.

I am here for Him and He is there for me.

I tell Him what I need and He tells me what He wants. Sometimes I finish what He started and other times He finishes what I started.

He takes responsibility for what I do and I take responsibility for what He does.

Sometimes He takes over from where I left off and sometimes I take over from where He left off.

When He moves I move and when He stops I stop and sometimes He moves when I move and stops when I stop.

He put me here for those who want to fight Him, if they defeat me on a levelled field they can consider themselves to have defeated Him.

I am my own Prophet

If prophethood was not ended I would have been the prophet of my time but I could still be an honorary prophet like the hadith says (anyone who carries the Quran in his chest has gained himself prophethood but he doesn't receive revelation to convey to people). I got what it takes and was given the ability to speak for Allah.

I know who is a believer and who's not, whether the person in front of me is of the people of hell or paradise.

I am the messenger of Allah to myself, my spirit is the messenger to myself and ego.

When I am with people I am Adam, when I meet religious people I become Ibrahim, amongst Muslims I am Ismail, when I live with unbelievers I am Yusuf, if I meet the rich and powerful I become Moses, in worshipping Allah I become David, when I deal with satans I become Suleiman (Solomon), when the world closes on me I become Yunus (Jonah) when I have no children I become Zakariya, when I am ill I become Ayub (Job) when I am with my parents I am Yahya (John) when I meet the Dajjal I become Jesus, when I meet the enemies of Allah I am Muhammad.

Allah believes in me and I believe in Him, He leans on me and I lean on Him, when He walks I walk and when He stops I stop and sometimes when I walk He walks and when I stop He stops.

When I want to say something to somebody He tells them on my behalf and when He wants to say something to somebody I do it on His behalf.

Sometimes when He wants to go somewhere He sends me there first and sometimes when I want to go somewhere He goes there for me first.

He created this universe for me and created me for Himself.

I make peace for Him and He goes to war for me.

He'll swap me with mankind.

He is the dangerous aspect about me.

I gave Him everything I have and don't have and He gave me everything He has.

* I don't act upon or do anything according to anything I wrote here so don't take anything I said seriously, these thoughts are nothing but self-esteem that got out of control a little bit, they just come to my mind and go but help me get through the day, otherwise I am just a human being like everyone else and may the peace and the mercy and the blessings of Allah be upon you Wa salamu allaikum wa rahmatu Allahi wa barakatu.

Your brother

Ibin Marriam

with my parents I am Yahya (John) when I meet the Dajjal I become Jesus, when I meet the enemies of Allah I am Muhammad.

Allah believes in me and I believe in Him, He leans on me and I lean on Him, when He walks I walk and when He stops I stop and sometimes when I walk He walks and when I stop He stops.

When I want to say something to somebody He tells them on my behalf and when He wants to say something to somebody I do it on His behalf.

Sometimes when He wants to go somewhere He sends me there first and sometimes when I want to go somewhere He goes there for me first.

He created this universe for me and created me for Himself.

I make peace for Him and He goes to war for me.

He'll swap me with mankind.

He is the dangerous aspect about me.

I gave Him everything I have and don't have and He gave me everything He has.

* I don't act upon or do anything according to anything I wrote here so don't take anything I said seriously, these thoughts are nothing but self-esteem that got out of control a little bit, they just come to my mind and go but help me get through the day, otherwise I am just a human being like everyone else and may the peace and the mercy and the blessings of Allah be upon you Wa salamu allaikum wa rahmatu Allahi wa barakatu.

Your brother

Ibin Marriam

www.ingramcontent.com/pod-product-compliance
Lightning Source LLC
Chambersburg PA
CBHW030043100526
44590CB00011B/320